THE WHY EFFECT: DRIVING SUCCESS THROUGH PURPOSEFUL LEADERSHIP

WENDY A. JOHNSON

Introduction

The Essence of Purposeful Leadership

Welcome to "The Why Effect: Driving Success Through Purposeful Leadership." The occupation of organization has never been more fundamental or so troublesome in a period of fast change, intricacy, and weakness. In the midst of this establishment, cognizant association arises as a historic way of thinking, offering pioneers a compass to explore intricacies, convince others, and drive conceivable achievement.

Understanding and aligning with one's "why," or the underlying values, motivations, and aspirations that drive meaningful action, is examined in this book, which delves into the core of purposeful leadership. Through an expansive assessment of fundamental standards, important methodologies, legitimate sensible assessments, and future models, perusers are outfitted with the information, experiences, and instruments expected to encourage deliberate drive inside themselves and their affiliations.

From uncovering individual clarification and changing get-togethers to authoritative focuses to examining inconveniences, utilizing advancement, and driving predictable improvement, each section offers endless snippets of data and essential heading. Whether you are a confident head hoping to foster purposeful practices or a carefully pre-arranged pioneer hoping to fabricate your impact, this book gives a manual for driving accomplishment, empowering responsibility, and having a critical effect in the current mind boggling and interconnected world.

Oblige us on this urgent excursion as we look at the force of intentional drive and find how concurring with your "why" can open inconspicuous breaking point, stir others, and make a helping through custom of productive result and satisfaction.

Chapter 1

Outline of Significant Administration

- Deciding the Objective and Its Impact

This segment explores the idea of direction and the huge manners by which it impacts authority viability. We examine how importance is a fundamental part that drives bosses to move, rouse, and accomplish long stretch accomplishment, going past direct goals or targets.

- The Significance of "Why" in Driving

This article looks at how huge it is for trailblazers to know and convey their "why" to lead effectively. This part emphasizes that it is a seriously big deal to organize approaches to acting with motivation to propel trust, responsibility, and various leveled insight. It does this by investigating mental pieces of information and authentic models.

This prologue to deliberate authority makes way for ensuing conversations of essential ideas, self-revelation, and hierarchical arrangement to work with a more top to bottom examination.

Chapter 2

Significant Contemplations

- The Headway of Speculation of Organization

This portion charts the headway of power hypotheses from standard moderate models to current procedures highlighting moral issues, reason, and collaboration. Perusers can sort out how deliberate authority deviates from or creates past frameworks by comprehending the genuine establishment.

- The Basics of Huge Power

Here, we spread out the central convictions of purposeful power, including sympathy, vision, and dependability. This portion figures out how trailblazers could propel followership, handle difficulties, and gain prudent headway by agreeing with these basic statutes through portrayed models and feasible contemplations.

This party outfits pursuers with a middle understanding of deliberate drive by examining both the evident development and key considerations. This prepares for extra assessment of individual disclosure, various leveled game plans, transparent;" so, practical execution.

Chapter 3

Finding and Expressing Your Main goal

- Techniques for Deciding Your Own "Why"

This part covers various techniques and exercises intended to help individuals in finding their own "why." Perusers are taken on a changing excursion to find the basic convictions, intentions, and goals that decide their motivation through canny activities, reflection questions, and genuine stories.

- Compelling Reason Correspondence

In this article, we investigate the workmanship and study of successfully and truly conveying one's motivation. Creating a compelling purpose statement, utilizing narrative tools, and motivating others by speaking with authenticity and conviction are all covered in this section.

This part assists perusers to interface their own qualities with their positions of authority, which advances genuineness, commitment, and huge effect inside their groups and associations. It does this by accentuating both the disclosure and enunciation parts of the cycle.

Chapter 4

Creating Organizations with a Purpose

- Matching Gatherings to the Target of the Association

This part digs into strategies for planning offices and groups with the association's general objective. Perusers are shown how to foster a typical vision, put forth unambiguous objectives, and urge cooperation that prompts bunch achievement and satisfaction through contextual investigations, best practices, and helpful bits of knowledge.

- Encouraging a Purposeful Culture

Here, we take a gander at the fundamental parts expected to encourage a purposeful culture inside an organization. This segment investigates hierarchical designs, correspondence strategies, and administration ways of behaving that help values-driven independent direction, worker commitment, and arrangement with reason.

This section gives supervisors and chiefs the information and assets they need to construct associations that achieve their essential objectives as well as persuade and empower individuals to make critical commitments to a shared objective by underlining arrangement and culture supporting.

Chapter 5

Overcoming Obstacles with a Purpose

- Variety and Strength Techniques

This fragment dives into the techniques used by conscious trailblazers to beat hindrances, weakness, and frustrations sincerely and versatility. Perusers will get significant considerations and authentic models that help them with staying fixed on their "why," change setbacks into showing minutes, and guide their gatherings through times of weakness and change.

- Staying away from Normal Authority Traps

In this part, we recognize and examine normal administration entanglements that pioneers might experience while endeavoring to become deliberate pioneers. To help pioneers with staying dedicated to their focal objective and values, this part gives logical gadgets, intelligent activities, and even minded deals with any consequences regarding address obstructions like recklessness, misalignment, and moral issues.

This segment gives spearheads the information and limits they need to organize complex conditions, develop conviction and trust among accomplices, and stay consistent with their inspiration notwithstanding inevitable difficulties and weaknesses by underlining flexibility, variety, and hazards.

Chapter 6

Managing Effective Teams

- Methodologies for Recruiting and Advancement

In the process of deliberate administration, this section discusses reasonable methods for gathering, preparing, and encouraging successful groups. Perusers are given utilitarian encounters, context oriented investigations, and best practices to help them with finding people who share the affiliation's vision, encourage capacity, and give improvement and headway astounding entryways.

- Rousing Gatherings with an Objective

In this segment, we look at how deliberate pioneers engage their staff by interfacing individual positions and obligations to the association's bigger objective. This portion gives steady direction in how to support partner responsibility, effectiveness, and happiness by enabling freedom, facilitated exertion, and a sense of satisfaction.

In this part, selecting and headway procedures and reinforcing methodologies are analyzed comprehensively. This gives bosses the devices and information they need to make and supervise high-performing bunches that help the targets, values, and justification behind their affiliation.

Chapter 7

Assessing and Improving Leadership with a Purpose

- Rules for Looking over Deliberate Impact

We look at assessments and key execution markers (KPIs) in this part to assist pioneers with reviewing the impacts of cognizant association in their affiliations. Perusers get wise bearing, setting focused examinations, and reliable devices to assist them with surveying plan, obligation, and other enormous bits of heading driven achievement.

- Examination Structures and Solid Improvement

Here, we look at techniques for empowering an examination driven and dependably further making society inside cognizant drive practices. This part gives data on the most skilled methodology to fabricate investigation circles, get input from accessories, and use data to also cultivate game-plan, make steady movement, and sharpen drive procedures.

This section outfits pioneers with the gadgets, frameworks, and snippets of data indispensable to review their impact, pinpoint areas for progress, and steadily work on their strategy for deliberate ability to make extended length progress and conclusive sensibility. It does this by featuring evaluation and overhaul.

Chapter 8

Case Studies of Leadership with a Purpose

- Authentic Cases of Achievements Driven by Reason

This part takes a gander at certifiable relevant investigations of bosses and associations that have really executed deliberate organization frameworks. Perusers get basic snippets of data into how reason driven drives can impel innovative psyche, obligation, and extended length accomplishment through beginning to end appraisals, frames learned, and best practices.

- Activities from Drive Errors and Wins

In this part, we see pertinent assessments of moderate troubles, misalignments, and drive bumbles that typically circle back. This part remembers the significance of intentional master for managing intricacies, beating hardships, and moving strength by giving sincere snippets of data, expressive evaluations, and viable models gained from these encounters.

By focusing on the two victories and dissatisfactions, this part outfits pursuers with an expansive cognizance of the potential and difficulties related with purposeful drive. Pioneers are given the principal data, frameworks, and assets to truly investigate their particular conditions and accomplish their ideal objectives using authentic models and valuable experiences.

Chapter 9

Prospects and Concluding Remarks

- New Advancements and the Development of Initiative

This part dives into the manners in which state of the art advancements like computerized change, man-made consciousness, and information examination are affecting the bearing of deliberate authority later on. Perusers have a forward-looking point of view on the most proficient method to utilize innovation to further develop arrangement, commitment, and hierarchical accomplishment through bits of knowledge into evolving patterns, open doors, and issues.

- Remarks at the End: Keeping up with Objectives in a Changing Climate

All things being equal, we consider the immortal upsides of deliberate administration and their importance in a world that is continually developing. As innovation propels, society changes, and hierarchical elements change, this part gives shutting contemplations, reflections, and ideas for keeping up with reason, building strength, and producing significant effect.

This part finishes up the bits of knowledge, strategies, and thoughts talked about all through the book by focusing on future patterns and shutting considerations. In the wake of perusing this book, perusers will have a careful handle of deliberate initiative and be propelled to try these thoughts in their own specific circumstances to make achievement, satisfaction, and positive change in a world that is evolving rapidly.